S0-BNT-683

PARTNERS

BILL HANNA & BARBERA JOE

YABBA-DABBA-DOO!

BY

Laurie Rozakis

Illustrations by Dick Smolinski

A BLACKBIRCH PRESS BOOK

WOODBRIDGE, CONNECTICUT

Published by Blackbirch Press, Inc.
One Bradley Road
Woodbridge , CT 06525

©1994 Blackbirch Press, Inc.
First Edition

Printed in Hong Kong

10 9 8 7 6 5 4 3 2 1

Library of Congress Cataloging-in-Publication Data

Rozakis, Laurie.
    Hanna & Barbera: yabba-dabba-doo! / by Laurie Rozakis. —1st ed.
       p.   cm.
    Includes bibliographical references and index.
    ISBN 1-56711-065-7
    1. Hanna-Barbera Productions—Juvenile literature. 2. Animated
films—United States—Juvenile literature. [1. Hanna-Barbera Productions.
2. Animated films.] I. Title. II. Title: Hanna and Barbera.
NC1766.U52H3636   1994
791.45'092'2—dc20
                                                  93-42986
                                                     CIP
                                                       AC

°°° **Contents** °°°

The cartoon world of Bill Hanna and Joe Barbera is filled with hundreds of characters, including the Flintstones, Yogi Bear, and the Jetsons.

Let the Magic Begin!

Joe Barbera came from New York City. Bill Hanna lived in California. Joe was a banker, and Bill was an engineer. What could they have in common? A love of *cartoons*! They met for the first time in 1937, in the new Cartoon Department of MGM Studios in Culver City, California. At that time, they had no idea they would become the most famous team in cartoon history.

First they made more than 200 *Tom and Jerry* cartoons and won seven *Academy Awards*! Then came *Huckleberry Hound*, *Quick Draw McGraw*, *Yogi Bear*, *The Flintstones*, *Top Cat*, *The Jetsons*, and so many more great shows.

Smurfs, Pac-Man, and More

In 1957, Joe and Bill left MGM and formed their own company. They called it Hanna-Barbera Productions, Inc. The company, with its 800-plus workers, has made more than 150 cartoon series for television. Have you watched *The Flintstone Kids*, *Pound Puppies*, *The Biskitts*, *The Dukes*, *Pac-Man*, *The Smurfs*, or *Richie Rich*? These are all Hanna-Barbera shows. More than 500 million viewers

every week watch these cartoons. They are shown
around the world and are even in many different
languages in many different countries.

Joe Barbera and Bill Hanna Today

Joe Barbera has dark curly hair and a wide smile.
He and his wife, Sheila, have two daughters, Jayne
and Lynn, and a son, Neal. They also have two
grandchildren and two great-grandchildren. Bill
Hanna is a twinkly-eyed, white-haired man. He has
a square face and a deep *cleft,* or line, in his chin.
Very quiet, he rarely speaks to reporters. He lives
with his wife, Violet. They have a son, David, a
daughter, Bonnie, and seven grandchildren.

But how did the magic between Bill and Joe
begin? And what were these partners like when they
were young? Let's take a look at the early years of
these two men who shared the same dream.

**The Flintstones is one of the most
popular cartoons in television history.**

2

Joe Barbera

Joe Barbera was born in 1911, in New York City's Lower East Side. A few years before, his parents had sailed to America from Italy. While Joe was still a baby, his parents moved to the Flatbush section of Brooklyn. Joe's father liked to wear fancy suits and smoke big cigars. He also liked to bet money at the horse races. He had a good mind for business and bought three barber shops and beauty parlors. The Barbera family was warm and friendly.

A Happy Childhood

Many families that lived in Flatbush had come to America from other countries. The city streets were always crowded with children, and Joe had many friends. Back then, it was great to play on the streets. Horse-drawn carts loaded with good things would clip-clop down the alleys. To Joe, it seemed like peddlers sold everything from their carts! There were loaves of warm bread, piles of crisp vegetables, rows of shiny pots and pans, and heaps of new and used clothing. Joe Barbera's childhood world was very different from that of today. For example, refrigerators had not yet been invented, and people used boxes filled with ice to keep their food cold. These iceboxes looked like refrigerators, but the food was cooled with blocks of ice. On his cart, an iceman would stack big slabs of ice. When someone called to him, he would stop his horses in the middle of the street to chop off a big chunk.

The streets were fun and exciting, but young Joe had another interest: drawing.

The streets were fun and exciting, but young Joe had another interest. Joe liked to draw. On rainy days, he would spread magazines all over the floor and spend hours copying the drawings. The nuns who taught Joe at Holy Innocents Catholic School saw that Joe had a talent for art. They often asked him to draw simple religious scenes on the classroom blackboards.

Joe Barbera grew up in New York City during the 1920s and spent much of his time playing in the neighborhood streets.

After Joe graduated, he went to Public School 139 on Cortelyou Road. After that, he went to Erasmus Hall High School. There, the teachers saw that he was as good at writing as he was at drawing! One day, his English teacher asked him to make up a story. Joe was particularly interested in the fierce Russian soldiers called *cossacks*. It seemed like a good topic for a story, Joe thought. "The story was about cossacks attacking a village, and it was all seen through the eyes of a wounded soldier," Joe recalls. The teacher was so pleased with the story that she asked him to read it to the class. Joe was happy about the honor.

Hard Times

When he was 16, Joe graduated from high school and the future looked bright. But just two years later, the economy in America would become ruined. In 1929, millions of people who had put their money into big companies lost everything. Hundreds of banks failed, and many factories, mills, and companies closed. By 1932, more than 10 million people were out of work, including Joe. Many Americans lost their homes. The *Great Depression*,

Whether he was drawing or writing, young Joe always used his rich imagination.

as this period was called, was so bad that its effects reached around the world.

After searching for months, Joe finally got a job. It wasn't in drawing, writing, or theater. The Irving Trust Company hired Joe to file income-tax returns—forms that show how much money people have

13

made during the year. Joe was talented in many things, but math was not one of them—he couldn't even add simple numbers. "To this day, they must be looking for my mistakes," he jokes. Joe didn't like the work at all. The best part of the job, he later said, were his lunch hours. Still, people did not quit a job—no matter how much they disliked it—in the middle of the Great Depression. Joe's mother needed his help, so he gave her part of the money he earned. What kept him going?

I Want to Draw!

Joe dreamed of making his own cartoons—but he also did more than dream. Every night he would draw cartoons, hoping that some magazine would use one. Once a week, during his lunch hour, he'd race uptown on the subway to drop off his cartoons on the doorsteps of *Redbook*, *Collier's*, *The New Yorker*, and *The Saturday Evening Post*. But no one bought his cartoons, and the next week he would have to pick them all up and take them home again. This went on week after week. To sharpen his drawing skills, Joe started taking night classes at the famous Art Students League of Manhattan.

The Great Depression of the 1930s
left millions of Americans poor and
out of work.

Then one day a letter came from *Collier's* magazine. With it was a $25 check! *Collier's* had bought one of Joe's cartoons! He sold a few more cartoons to *Collier's*, but it didn't seem as though he could sell enough to support himself. He took more art classes at night while he continued working at Irving Trust Company during the day.

The Big Break?

When Joe was 19, he decided it was time to make a move. So he left the bank and started to work at Fleischer Studios. Max and Dave Fleischer, two brothers, were famous for their *Popeye the Sailor* and *Betty Boop* cartoons. At that time, all cartoons were painted by hand on sheets of *celluloid*, a see-through material. Joe was hired to paint these sheets of celluloid, called *cels*, and he was paid $35 a week. This was a lot of money in those days. Joe also got paid $1 for every joke of his that was used in a cartoon. This job seemed like his big break.

But after only four days, Joe decided that the job was not right. He left Fleischer Studios and asked for his job back at the bank. But the bank could not hire him back. Joe tried to be cheerful, but he was

Joe's big break came when he got a job as a cartoon artist at the Van Beuren Studio in New York.

very upset. He could not support himself, and he didn't have any money to give to his mother.

Then Joe got really lucky. He met a friend from high school who said, "There's a job for a cartoonist at the Van Beuren Studio." That company was in Manhattan, across the street from Max Fleischer's studio. Van Beuren Studio was not famous, or even well known, but Joe thought it might be the right place for him to learn about making cartoons. After all, he had worked in cartoons for only four days!

Joe applied for the job and got it. For six months, he worked night and day. Like a sponge, Joe soaked up all he could about making cartoons. He learned about drawing cartoon figures, painting the cels, and writing *scripts.* Joe was so happy. He loved his work and was sure that he had found a job for life.

> *In 1936, cartoonist Paul Terry invited Joe to work at his studio.*

Terrytoons

In 1936, Van Beuren went out of business, so once again, Joe had to look for a job. He decided there was only one place to make cartoons—at Walt Disney's studio in California. A few years before, he had sent Disney some cartoons and a letter. Mr. Disney had not answered, but Joe was desperate. He packed up to move to California. Before he got on the train, however, Joe went to Paul Terry's cartoon studio in New Rochelle, New York, to say good-bye to some of his friends. As he was leaving, Joe met Mr. Terry himself. Terry was well known for his *Terrytoon* cartoons. Later, he would create *Mighty Mouse* and *Heckle and Jeckle.* Believe it or not, Terry offered Joe a job right on the spot. Joe Barbera was back in the cartoon business.

3

Bill Hanna

William Denby Hanna was born in 1910 at the opposite end of the country from Joe Barbera—in Melrose, New Mexico. His father helped build the Santa Fe railroads. Every time Mr. Hanna finished one train stop, the family would move on to the next one. Since Mr. Hanna worked pretty fast, Bill moved a lot when he was a child. By the time Bill was three years old, the family was living in Baker, Oregon. This time, his father was building a dam. Bill liked living in Baker. He used to visit the dam to watch his father work. There were so many trout in the water that people could lift the fish from the shallow

19

water with their bare hands. Bill sometimes got in trouble, too. Bill remembers one particular day when he and his sister Norma broke all the windows in the family's barn. They did it because they both liked the pretty pattern that the cracked glass made in the window frames.

Moving Around the Country

By the time Bill started school, the family had moved to Logan, Utah, where the winters were bitterly cold. Sometimes, students got frostbitten feet on their way to school, and the teacher had to rub their feet next to the hot iron stove until they warmed up. It was very painful. But Bill remembers good times, too, like sledding in the deep snow. In 1917, when Bill was seven years old, the family moved once more.

Growing up, Bill and his family lived in many places across the country.

This time, they went to San Pedro, California, where they stayed for two years. There was an army fort at San Pedro, and Bill liked to go to the fort to watch the soldiers practice shooting. He also spent hours looking at the houses the Oriental fishermen had built over the harbor.

After Bill's family moved to Los Angeles, California, in 1919, he became a Boy Scout.

In 1919, the Hannas moved to Los Angeles, California. When he was 12 years old, Bill joined the Boy Scouts. He liked being a Boy Scout so much that he is still active in scouting today. Young Bill also loved music. He started playing the saxophone and soon joined a neighborhood band. Later, he took piano lessons.

Work in Construction

When it was time for Bill to go to high school, the Hanna family was living in Compton, California. Bill's favorite subjects were *journalism* and math. He played many sports, too. After high school, Bill went to Compton Junior College, where he studied journalism and engineering. Because times were very bad during the Depression, however, he left college to find a job. Just like Joe Barbera, whom he would meet some years later, he had a hard time getting work. Finally, he found a job with a group of construction engineers who were building a large theater in Hollywood. When the theater was finished, though, Bill decided that he didn't like being an engineer. He knew it was time for him to move in a new direction.

Bitten by the "Cartoon Bug"

Bill heard about Harman-Ising Studios, a new cartoon studio. Working in a small room above a dress shop, Hugh Harman and Rudy Ising created *Looney Tunes* and *Merrie Melodies* cartoons. Like Joe Barbera, Bill was put to work painting cels and doing other odd jobs. "My job was to run for coffee,

Joe had the chance to visit Hollywood when he helped some engineers build a theater there.

to wipe cels, to sweep up, and to drown my bosses with story ideas," he says. As the company grew, so did Bill's job. By the end of the first year, he was the head of a department and earned $37.50 a week. His boss, Rudy Ising, worked from noon to midnight seven days a week. Bill joined the late-night sessions. He also started writing stories and *gags* for the cartoons. Soon he was even writing music. For seven years, Bill worked happily with Harman-Ising.

In 1937, MGM hired Bill to run its animation department. Joe Barbera soon joined him.

Lightning Strikes!

Bill worked in all the major areas of cartoon making, which suited him just fine. But in 1937, the giant Hollywood film company MGM started its own cartoon studio. Suddenly, Culver City, California, was the best place for cartoonists to be. On June 7, MGM hired Bill to run its *animation* department, where cartoons were made. Within a few months, someone at the company contacted Joe Barbera, who joined MGM as a cartoon artist at $87.50 a week. With Bill and Joe both at MGM, the stage was set for the two men to meet.

4

Tom and Jerry

Joe and Bill got along from the start. Soon, they saw that they shared something special. Joe was great at writing jokes, and Bill wanted to be a director. Joe could draw like lightning. "He was the best cartoonist I'd ever seen," Bill recalls. And Bill could make a joke really funny. They knew they were a perfect team, but somehow they had to prove it to the boss. In order to do that, their first cartoon would have to be a winner.

25

We Need an Idea!

They tried a lot of ideas, but nothing seemed right. After many false starts, they came up with two typical enemies—a cat and a mouse. Everyone knows that cats chase mice—and usually catch them! With a cat and a mouse in it, the cartoon would have many wild chases—and the mouse would have lots of near escapes. Working far into the night, Joe and Bill created their first cartoon, called *Puss Gets the Boot.*

There was no television yet in the 1930s, so people went to the movies a lot. Before movies started, cartoons were shown. The cartoon that Bill and Joe created, they hoped, would become popular with movie audiences.

A Game of Cat and Mouse

Puss Gets the Boot starred a house cat named Jasper and a mouse who was never named. Jasper was very clumsy. He would break many things around the house as he chased the mouse. Whenever the housekeeper warned him that he would be kicked out of the house if he broke one more thing, the mouse saw it as his chance to get back at the cat. The mouse would tease Jasper and threaten to break

a glass if Jasper came any closer. Who won the bat-
tle in the end? The mouse!   Jasper is thrown out of
the house and the happy mouse puts a "Home Sweet
Home" sign above his mouse hole.

   Puss Gets the Boot was a huge hit. It was even
up for an Academy Award, although it didn't get
one. A bit later, Bill and Joe thought more about the
cat Jasper and the mouse. Nobody liked the name
Jasper much. And the mouse didn't even have a
name. Finally, MGM decided to hold a contest
to find names. All the cartoonists tossed
names into a hat. Bill and Joe picked
"Tom" for the cat and "Jerry" for the
mouse, and the winner got $50.

Bill and Joe's first project together, Puss Gets the Boot, starred a clever mouse and a clumsy cat named Jasper.

A Winning Team

Bill and Joe would make *Tom and Jerry*
cartoons for the next 20 years. "We
breathed, ate, slept cartoons," they remember. They
changed the way the cat and mouse looked, but the
stories stayed the same. Tom was always chasing
Jerry—and rarely catching him!

   Although the cat seemed eager to get the mouse,
people knew that Tom and Jerry really didn't want to

Bill and Joe worked together as a team producing *Tom and Jerry* cartoons for 20 years.

hurt each other. In *The Night Before Christmas*, Tom worries that Jerry will freeze in the cold. In *Nit Witty Kitty*, Jerry loses his memory and Tom works hard to help him get it back. In *Just Ducky*, Jerry feeds hot soup to a freezing Tom.

Bill and Joe worked hard on every step together. Bill acted out all the scenes, every single gag. That helped Joe draw exactly what they needed. It took the two men and their helpers six weeks to make a seven-minute cartoon. Then they added beautiful music and wild sound effects. It cost $30,000 per cartoon—more than $4,000 per minute. That was a lot of money in the 1940s and 1950s.

Laughs and More Laughs

The *Tom and Jerry* cartoons won seven Academy Awards. That was more than any other cartoon series. Joe and Bill were pleased with the honors, but they were even happier that Tom and Jerry made people happy. "The gags brought laughs from beginning to end. That was our reward," they explain. The good feelings were another reward. Everyone at the MGM animation department worked well with one another.

Over the years, the Tom and Jerry *cartoons won seven Academy Awards.*

The two partners were also a lot of fun to be around. One day Joe drilled a hole in the wall where an artist had a habit of resting his head. He ran a soda straw through the hole. Then, when he

Bill and Joe always had a lot of fun at the office and would often play jokes on their fellow workers.

saw that the artist was sitting at his desk, he filled his mouth with water and squirted it through the straw at the artist's head! But the artist got back at Joe. He filled a big film can with water and put it above Joe's desk. He wrapped a string around the can and

tied it to an electric fan. When Joe turned the fan on, the string pulled down the can of water. Joe stepped back just in time. "The whole business was fun. It was hard work, but it was fun," remembers an artist. But would it stay fun forever?

∘∘∘ 5 ∘∘∘

An Empire Built on Laughter

By the end of the 1950s, Joe and Bill had a secure place at MGM. They were making eight cartoons a year, and the quality stayed as high as ever. They were also winning awards. But there were now new problems brewing.

MGM was in trouble. Costs had gone up and people were going to the movies less. Now many people stayed home and watched a new invention: television. In 1957, MGM closed its cartoon studio. "Here we were thinking that we're at the top of the heap," Joe remembers. "Without a hint, the phone rings. 'Close the studio! Lay everybody off!'" Bill and Joe went to every studio looking for work, but no one was making cartoons. They just cost too much. It seemed as if their dream was over.

32

Down but Not Out

Bill and Joe had worked together for 20 years and wanted to continue. As soon as the studio closed, they started thinking of new characters. They created a sweet but dopey dog named Ruff and a smart cat named Reddy. Unlike Tom and Jerry, Ruff and Reddy would be friends. They would also talk. Joe made the drawings, and his daughter Jayne colored them. Over and over, the project was turned down. But then Joe and Bill got lucky again.

In the fall of 1957, Screen Gems hired Bill and Joe to make a five-minute *Ruff and Reddy* cartoon for television. Things didn't go well at first. The boss took one look at the cartoon and shouted, "Get rid of them! Just drop the whole idea!" Then they came to an agreement: Each cartoon could cost only $3,000. At that time, the average cartoon cost $30,000. How could Joe and Bill stick to this tough budget? They created a new kind of animation! They called it "planned" animation. Instead of 1,000 drawings, it used just 300. The cartoon lost some of its rich detail, but lots of money was saved. In this way, Joe and Bill actually made television cartoons possible.

As soon as *Ruff and Reddy* was a hit, Joe and Bill did a lot of smart things. First, they started their own company. They hired all the best cartoonists and musicians they could find, and they found the perfect actors to do the voices. Next, they made all the cartoons in color, even though they were shown in black-and-white at first. "It was one of the smartest things we did," Bill recalls. "Color will be here soon," he said. "Cartoons last forever. Let's go ahead and do them in color, and we'll be a jump ahead of the game."

A Dog and a Bear Team Up

The time seemed to be right for a half-hour cartoon program. To do this, Bill and Joe created a happy but silly dog. They considered calling him "Alfalfa Hound," "Cactus Hound," and "Dingy Dog." But finally the partners settled on Huckleberry Hound. They added a cute cat named Mr. Jinx and the mice he chased, Dixie and Pixie. But the third character was the biggest hit of all. That character was a bear who lives in Jellystone National Park and steals "pic-a-nic" baskets from the visitors. He also has a bear-cub pal named Boo Boo. His name is Yogi Bear.

Yogi Bear was one of Bill and Joe's first major successes on their own.

Right from the start—October 2, 1958—*The Huckleberry Hound Show*, with the goofy, funny dog and the cagey bear, was a big hit. Soon *The Huckleberry Hound Show* became the first cartoon to win an *Emmy Award* for its outstanding achievement in children's programming.

Soon after, Bill and Joe created many other familiar characters. Among them was a mustang horse from New Mexico called Quick Draw McGraw and his partner, the Mexican burro Baba Looey. "Hold on thar!" Quick Draw often shouted. "I'll do all the thinkin' around here. . . and don-o-n't you forget it!"

Yabba-dabba-doo!

By 1960, Joe and Bill had proved that animation could work on television. Their shows were on more than 100 television stations, and they were on in the early evening, when mostly children would be watching. Then Joe and Bill had a wild idea. What about a cartoon show for adults?

They knew they wanted the show to make fun of modern life. They dressed the characters in modern clothes. That didn't work. Next they tried togas— long loose clothing worn by ancient Romans. Nope.

They tried Pilgrims. What about the Stone Age?
They loved it! And that's how *The Flintstones* was
born! The first show aired on September 30, 1960.
Fred, Wilma, and Pebbles Flintstone were the stars,
along with their neighbors, Barney, Betty, and Bamm
Bamm Rubble. *The Flintstones* ran for six years and
won many awards—and many fans.

**When Joe and
Bill decided to
produce a car-
toon that adults
would like,
they created
The Flintstones.**

From Stone Age to Space Age

The Flintstones took place in the past. Where would
Bill and Joe go next? To the future, of course! The
twenty-first century, to be exact. In 1962, *The
Jetsons* zoomed onto television. George Jetson, his

37

Hanna-Barbera Productions followed up its super success with *The Flintstones* by creating a space-age family called the Jetsons.

wife, Jane, their children, Judy and Elroy, and Astro the dog, all lived in a skypad apartment in Orbit City. Like *The Flintstones*, the show ran for six years and it is still seen in *reruns* today. It got more laughs than any other Hanna-Barbera production. "That show was ahead of its time," Joe recalls. In the years that followed, Hanna-Barbera created lots of other great new shows: *Lippy the Lion*, *Touché Turtle*, *Magilla Gorilla*, *Atom Ant*, and *Secret Squirrel,* to name a few.

The Superheroes and Other New Shows

In the 1960s, astronauts like Gordon Cooper, Alan Shepard, and John Glenn were soaring into space. For Bill and Joe, it was time to look to the comic-book heroes of their childhood. "As kids, Bill and I had always loved the big heroic figures like Tom Swift. Now it was our turn to create our own," Joe says. In 1964, they launched *The Adventures of Johnny Quest.* This action-adventure show was a big hit. Then came more series: *Space Ghost, Dino Boy, Shazzan,* and *The Fantastic Four.*

In 1968, CBS, ABC, and NBC decided to buy brand-new cartoons for Saturday morning. Up to

that point, they had been using only reruns. Within
months, Bill and Joe were making one third of these
new cartoons. Their new projects included
*Penelope Pitstop, Wacky Races, Danger
Island*, and *Scooby-Doo, Where Are You?*

Animated Specials

In the 1970s, Joe and Bill started making
full-length movies around their most popular characters. Many mixed real people with
cartoon characters. They began with famous children's books: *Alice in Wonderland, Gulliver's
Travels, Black Beauty, Charlotte's Web*, and *Jack and
the Beanstalk*. *Newsweek* magazine called their
movies "heartwarming." *The Village Voice*, a New
York City newspaper, said the films were "terrific."

By the 1980s, Bill and Joe were taking popular
television shows and making them into cartoons:
*Fonz and the Happy Days Gang, Laverne and
Shirley*, and *Mork and Mindy*. During this time period, they also developed *The Smurfs*, which won two
Emmy Awards. And from one of the first popular
video games, Hanna-Barbera got the idea for their
successful *Pac-Man* cartoon.

In the 1970s, Joe and Bill started making full-length movies.

Still Hard at Work

Today, Bill and Joe are still working on many new ideas, some with Andrew Lloyd Weber. Weber is the famous British composer who created the musical *Cats* and the Broadway version of *Phantom of the Opera*. Weber and Hanna-Barbera want to mix animation with live action. Bill and Joe have also teamed up with Steven Spielberg, who created *Raiders of the Lost Ark* and *Indiana Jones and the Temple of Doom*. They have worked together with comedians, too, like Lily Tomlin, Rodney Danger-field, and Whoopi Goldberg.

Awards and Rewards

Together, Joe and Bill have won many awards. In 1985, the Boy Scouts gave Bill the Distinguished Eagle Scout Award for 60 years in scouting. The same year, Joe got the Columbian Award from the Federated Italo-Americans of Southern California. In 1988, the National Academy of Television Arts and Sciences awarded both men the Governor's Award. Bill and Joe are especially proud of their "Laugh Rooms"—special hospital rooms where sick children can have fun and forget they are sick for awhile.

In the past 50 years, many things have changed in the way cartoons are made. People no longer paint cels by hand. Most work is done by computers. The computer has codes for the characters' movements, like eye blinks, shock vibrations, and nods. Today, Hanna-Barbera Productions is a very big company, and it now spends millions just to make one cartoon feature. But some things never change. Joe and Bill feel most proud when people tell them how much pleasure their television series have brought to them during the past 30 years. "I have a simple goal," Joe says. "It is to make people laugh." Their gift to us? The magic of laughter!

Together, Bill and Joe have won many important awards. In 1988, the National Academy of Television Arts and Sciences presented them with the distinguished Governor's Award.

43

Glossary

Academy Award An award given to a person who works in the motion-picture industry.

animation A motion picture made by photographing successive positions of still objects, such as cartoon characters.

cartoon In the motion-picture industry, a type of movie whose characters are not real people and whose object is to make the audience laugh.

celluloid A see-through material on which cartoons were once drawn. The sheets of celluloid were called *cels* for short.

cleft A line or crack.

cossacks Russian soldiers who fought on horseback.

Emmy Award An award given to a person who works in television.

gag A trick that is played on someone to make people laugh.

Great Depression A period in the 1930s when many people were out of work and times were generally hard.

journalism The study that deals with newspaper and magazine reporting.

rerun A re-presentation of a movie or television program after it has been shown, or run, for the first time.

script A written guideline for a show such as a movie, television program, or cartoon. It has the words the characters will say and the directions for music and sound effects.

Further Reading

Benjamin, Carol L. *Cartooning for Kids.* New York: HarperCollins Publishers, 1982.

Byars, Betsy. *The Cartoonist.* New York: Dell Publishing Company, 1981.

Edwards, R. Scott and Bob Stobener. *Cel Magic: The Book on Collecting Animation Art.* Sacramento, CA: Laughs Unlimited, 1990.

Gautier, Dick. *The Career Cartoonist: A Step-by-Step Guide to Presenting and Selling Your Artwork.* New York: The Putnam Publishing Group, 1992.

Hodge, Anthony. *Cartooning.* New York: Franklin Watts, 1992.

Jenkins, Patrick. *Animation.* Redding, MA: Addison-Wesley Publishing, 1991.

Index